Outside the station, Mr. Bear looked round him. He saw a band playing in front of a splendid house. "That looks nice," he thought and walked over to have a look. To his surprise a rabbit in a red jacket came forward and led him straight inside.

The rabbit seated Mr. Bear at a table.
Then other rabbits, also in red jackets,
brought him dish after dish of
the most delicious food.
"How very kind they are,"
thought Mr. Bear. "I must eat
everything or they will think
I am not enjoying myself."

When he had finished, he thanked the rabbits for his meal and got up to leave. A lady rabbit at a table near the door spoke to him rather excitedly. Another rabbit in a tall white hat started to speak loudly into a telephone. Mr. Bear looked at them in surprise, then walked out into the street.

As soon as Mr. Bear appeared in the street, two rabbits in uniform took him by the arm.

They led him to a large lorry. "What a splendid welcome," thought Mr. Bear. He bowed politely to the crowds as they drove through the streets. Finally they all arrived in front of a large building.

Inside the building, the uniformed rabbits sat Mr. Bear down on two chairs. Other important looking rabbits started to talk. “These must be speeches of welcome,” thought Mr. Bear. He listened politely, though he could not understand a word. The rabbits were really saying that Mr. Bear must go to prison, because he had eaten in a restaurant and not paid the bill. Poor Mr. Bear had not understood.

But even when they put him in a prison cell Mr. Bear felt perfectly happy. "I suppose this is a hotel," he said to himself. "These rabbits are certainly very kind to me."

Next morning the prison warders set Mr. Bear to work in the prison vegetable garden. Mr. Bear really enjoyed himself. He dug and hoed and raked as hard as *three* Mr. Bears.

"I wonder how they knew I liked gardening?" he asked himself.

Mr. Bear did so much work that day that the rabbit warders decided to let him out of prison. They even gave him a sack of vegetables to take away with him.

Mr. Bear was delighted. “I will take some to the kind rabbits who gave me supper yesterday evening,” he said to himself.

When they saw Mr. Bear walk in through the door, the rabbits in the restaurant were very frightened.
"He must be angry because we sent him to prison," they said to each other.

Mr. Bear was not angry. He emptied out his vegetables and gave an armful of the best ones to the rabbit in the tall white hat.

"Thank you for that lovely meal yesterday," he said.

"He did not know he had to pay," thought the rabbit. "Well let's be friends now."

Then the owner of the restaurant
gave Mr. Bear his tall white hat.
They shook hands and sat down
to supper together
in the friendliest way.